CHRISTIAN BLANCK

CHILD HOOD HEROES

365 TOY CARS

"THE LOVE FOR CARS
STARTS IN THE NURSERY."

Ford Escort
Siku, 1972

1
JAN

VW Käfer Ovali
Dinky Toys, 2015 (Replica)

2
JAN

VW Bulli T1 Police
Siku, 1965

3
JAN

Wild Life Truck
Matchbox Superfast, 1978

4
JAN

Fiat 127
Majorette, 1975

5
JAN

Jenson Interceptor
Corgi Toys Rockets, 1969

6
JAN

Rascal Road Roller
Corgi Toys, 1970

7
JAN

Mercury Commuter / Ford Zodiac MK IV
Matchbox Superfast / By Lesney, 1971 / 1967

8
JAN

Mercedes-Benz 600 Pullmann
Corgi Toys, 1963

9
JAN

Porsche 911 Police
Siku, 1969

10
JAN

Dodge Wreck Truck Service
Majorette, 1968

11
JAN

Ford Transit Station Wagon
Siku, 1967

12
JAN

Citroën CX
Matchbox Superfast, 1980

13
JAN

Jeep Cherokee
Majorette, 1979

14
JAN

VW Käfer Desert Patrol

15

JAN

VW T2 Bulli
Majorette, 1976

16
JAN

VW Passat
Schuco, 1978

17
JAN

Aston Martin DB5 / DAF Truck
Corgi Toys / Matchbox, 1964 / 1971

18
JAN

Hairy Hustler
Matchbox by Lesney, 1971

19
JAN

VW LT 28
Siku, 1982

20
JAN

Ford 2 Door
Hot Wheels, 1982

21
JAN

Plymouth Grand Fury Police
Majorette, 1970

22
JAN

Merryweather Marquis Fire Engine
By Lesney, 1959

23
JAN

Racing Porsche 935
Matchbox, 1978

24
JAN

VW Bulli T1
Playart, 1967

25
JAN

VW Golf I
Siku, 1977

26
JAN

Three-Wheel Roller
Siku, 1969

27
JAN

Renault 16
Corgi Toys, 1969

28
JAN

VW K70
Schuco, 1970

29
JAN

Porsche 911
Siku, 1973

30
JAN

Mercedes-Benz Fire Truck Metz DL
Siku, 1966

31
JAN

Citroën 2CV
Maisto, 1988

1
FEB

VW Bulli T1
Matchbox by Lesney, 1965

2
FEB

Ford Kennel Pick-up Truck
Matchbox by Lesney, 1968

3
FEB

Batmobile
Corgi Toys Juniors, 1978

4
FEB

Ferrari Berlinetta 275 GTB
Siku, 1970

5
FEB

Citroën DS 21 Ambulance
Majorette, 1975

6
FEB

GMC Sierra Grande
Ertl, 1988

7
FEB

Maserati Boomerang
Siku, 1974

8
FEB

BMW M1
Matchbox, 1981

9
FEB

Porsche 356 Police
Märklin, 1963

10
FEB

Mercedes-Benz 500 SEC AMG
Matchbox, 1984

11
FEB

Renault 4L
Majorette, 1980

12
FEB

Peugeot 205 Turbo
Matchbox, 1984

13
FEB

Porsche 911 Turbo
Siku, 1983

14
FEB

Ford Transit
Siku, 1971

15
FEB

Fiat 500

16
FEB

Hot Rod Custom Van
Corgi Toys, 1984

17
FEB

VW Käfer 1200
Märklin, 1965

18
FEB

Wreck Truck
Matchbox by Lesney, 1968

19
FEB

VW 1500
Gama, 1969

20
FEB

Mercedes-Benz 250 SE
Siku, 1969

21
FEB

Ford Granada 3.0 MK I
Schuco, 1973

22
FEB

Fork Lift Truck
Matchbox Superfast, 1972

23
FEB

VW Bus T2 Speed Trap
Siku, 1974

24
FEB

Oldsmobile Toronado
Siku, 1969

25
FEB

Renault 5 Turbo
Majorette, 1985

26
FEB

Mercedes-Benz Limousine
Majorette, 1990

27
FEB

Unknown Model

28

FEB

Mercedes-Benz Fire Truck
Siku, 1987

29
FEB

Porsche 911 Targa
Darda Motor, 1988

1
MAR

Hot Rod Draguar
Matchbox by Lesney, 1970

2
MAR

Opel Diplomat
By Lesney, 1967

3
MAR

BMW Turbo
Schuco, 1972

4
MAR

VW Bulli T2 Flatbed Truck
Siku, 1975

5
MAR

Mercedes Truck No. 1
Matchbox by Lesney Superfast

6
MAR

Lincoln Continental
Matchbox by Lesney Superfast, 1973

7
MAR

Porsche 911 Turbo Cabriolet
Siku, 1987

8
MAR

Mercedes-Benz 250 SE/8
Siku, 1974

9
MAR

Bulldozer
Matchbox, 1983

10
MAR

Tomaso Pantera
Matchbox by Lesney, 1975

11
MAR

VW Käfer 1500 Saloon / Trailer
Matchbox Superfast / Majorette, 1976 / 1981

12
MAR

Airport Bus
Matchbox Superfast, 1977

13
MAR

Continental Mark III
Siku, 1970

14
MAR

VW Bucket Car
Siku, 1980

15
MAR

Ford Capri Police
Siku

16
MAR

Fiat 500
Vitesse

17
MAR

18

MAR

Nascar Pepsi Challenger Chevy Stock Car
Matchbox, 1984

Renault 5 TL
Matchbox Superfast, 1978

19
MAR

Sauber Group SHS C6 Racer
Matchbox, 1984

20
MAR

Volvo 12 Turbo / De Thomaso Mangusta
Siku / Corgi Toys, 1980 / 1970

21
MAR

Mercedes-Benz Silver Arrow
Märklin, 1953

22
MAR

K-21 Cougar Dragster
Matchbox by Lesney, 1970

23
MAR

Matchbox SS 100 Jaguar Cabriolet
Matchbox, 1982

24
MAR

VW Porsche 914 ADAC
Siku, 1977

25
MAR

Bedford Turntable Fire Escape Fire Truck
Dinky Supertoys, 1959

27
MAR

Matra-Simca Rancho
Siku, 1980

28
MAR

Mercury Cougar
Matchbox by Lesney, 1970

29
MAR

Porsche 924
Majorette, 1981

30
MAR

Citroën DS
Corgi Toys, 1960

31
MAR

SORRY!
TODAY
NO CAR

Double Vision
Hot Wheels, 1998

1
APR

Chevrolet Blazer Depanneuse
Majorette, 1986

2
APR

Volvo 240 DL
Majorette, 1976

3
APR

Audi 100 SL
Siku, 1974

4
APR

Porsche 928
Siku, 1983

5
APR

VW 1500 Station Wagon
Siku, 1967

6
APR

Jaguar E-Type
Matchbox by Lesney, 1966

7
APR

Petrol Truck
Matchbox, 1985

8
APR

VW Passat
Siku, 1981

9
APR

VW Käfer 1302 ADAC
Schuco, 1972

10
APR

Mercedes-Benz 200 Police
Schuco, 1970

11
APR

VW Porsche 911 Targa
Siku, 1978

12
APR

Bedford Tractor
Corgi Toys, 1959

13
APR

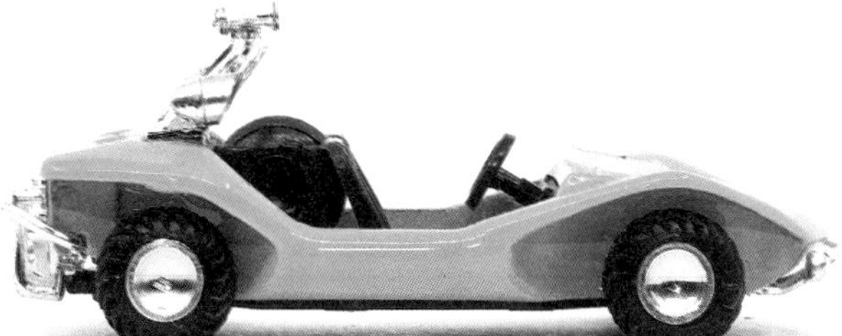

Pantone Buggy
Solido, 1971

14
APR

Range Rover
Siku, 1978

15
APR

Beetle Dragon Wheels
Matchbox by Lesney, 1972

16
APR

Maserati Bora
Matchbox by Lesney, 1972

17
APR

Saviem Tank Truck
Majorette, 1975

18
APR

Bond Bug
Corgi Toys Whizzlewheels, 1973

19
APR

Hot Rod Custom Van
Corgi Toys, 1984

20
APR

Toyota Pick-up 4×4
Majorette, 1982

21
APR

2000er Edition Michelin Citroën Typ H
Corgi Toys, 1958

22
APR

Porsche 911 Turbo
Schuco Toy Fair Limited Edition, 2015

23
APR

Ferrari P.5 Berlinetta
Politoys, 1968

24
APR

BMW 2000 CS Police
Siku, 1970

25
APR

Freeman Inter-City
Matchbox by Lesney, 1970

26
APR

Ford Mustang
Matchbox, 1966

27
APR

Mercedes-Benz Crane Truck
Siku, 1969

28
APR

VW Käfer 'Volksdragon'
Matchbox by Lesney, 1971

29
APR

Turbo Fury
Matchbox by Lesney, 1973

30
APR

AMX Javelin
Matchbox by Lesney, 1972

1
MAY

Sand Car Buggy
Matchbox Superkings Lesney, 1975

2
MAY

Krupp Titan LKW
Märklin, 1950

3
MAY

Porsche 917
Corgi Toys, 1973

4
MAY

VW Porsche 914
Schuco, 1978

5
MAY

K-6/11 Pick-up Truck
Matchbox by Lesney, 1974

6
MAY

Vauxhall Guildsman
Matchbox, 1971

7
MAY

Ford 17M Turnier ADAC
Siku, 1970

8
MAY

Renault 5 TL
Majorette, 1983

9
MAY

Jaguar E-Type
Majorette, 1977

10
MAY

Volkswagen 1600 TL
Matchbox by Lesney, 1969

11
MAY

Racing MINI Cooper S MK II
Matchbox by Lesney Superfast, 1970

12
MAY

Fiat 131 Abarth
Matchbox by Lesney, 1982

13
MAY

Ford Fireside Pick-Up
Hot Wheels, 1982

14
MAY

Buggy
Darda Motor, 1975

15
MAY

Ford Escort Typ II
Schuco, 1975

16
MAY

VW Bulli T1
Märklin, 1957

17
MAY

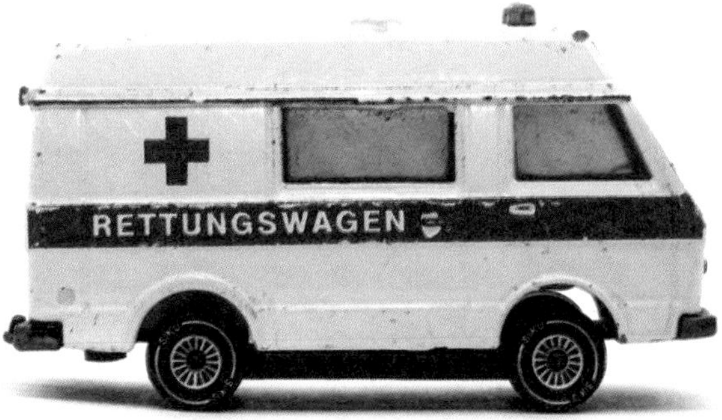

VW LT Ambulance
Siku, 1983

18
MAY

Henschel Aral Tank Truck
Siku, 1969

19
MAY

Setra Coach
Matchbox Superfast, 1970

20
MAY

Jaguar MK 10
By Lesney, 1964

21
MAY

Ford Tractor
Majorette, 1976

22
MAY

Rolls Royce Phantom V
Dinky Toys, 1965

23
MAY

Dodge Challenger
Matchbox by Lesney, 1975

24
MAY

Mercedes-Benz Unimog Ambulance
Siku, 1978

25
MAY

BMW CSI
Majorette, 1975

26
MAY

VW Golf 1 Cabriolet
Siku, 1980

27
MAY

Aston Martin DB5
Corgi Toys, 1965

28
MAY

VW Flying Bug
Matchbox by Lesney Superfast, 1972

29
MAY

Utility Truck
Matchbox, 1969

30
MAY

Jaguar E-Type
Corgi Toys Juniors, 1973

31
MAY

McLaren Ford
Yatming, 1980

1
JUN

VW Golf 2 GTI
Matchbox, 1985

2
JUN

Land Rover Safari
By Lesney, 1965

3
JUN

Mercedes-Benz 208
Siku, 1981

4
JUN

MGB GT
Corgi Toys, 1960

5
JUN

Jokermobile
Corgi Toys Juniors, 1981

6
JUN

MINI Ha-Ha
Matchbox by Lesney, 1975

7
JUN

Ford Transit Police
Siku, 1975

8
JUN

Greyhound Bus
Matchbox by Lesney, 1962

9
JUN

Fourgon VW
Majorette, 1975

10
JUN

Jeep
Matchbox by Lesney, 1973

11
JUN

Mercedes-Benz 'Binz' Ambulance
Matchbox by Lesney, 1970

12
JUN

Hanomag Henschel / Mercedes-Benz 250 Police
Siku, both 1974

13
JUN

Peugeot 504
Majorette, 1970

14
JUN

Gruesome Twosome
Matchbox by Lesney, 1971

15
JUN

Cadillac Ambulance
Matchbox by Lesney, 1965

16
JUN

Fire Engine Jeep
Matchbox

17
JUN

Rolls Royce Silver Shadow
Matchbox by Lesney, 1969

18
JUN

BMW 733
Majorette, 1984

19
JUN

Fiat 127 with trailer and boats
Majorette / Siku, 1972–2017

20
JUN

Ford Capri
Matchbox by Lesney, 1971

21
JUN

VW Käfer 1303
Tonka, 1975

22
JUN

Ford Truck
Corgi Toys, 1969

23
JUN

Ford Transit with kajak
Siku, 1974

24
JUN

Porsche 928
Matchbox, 1979

25
JUN

Ford Flareside Pick-up
Matchbox, 1982

26
JUN

BMW 633 CSI
Siku, 1981

27
JUN

Vauxhall Victor
By Lesney, 1963

28
JUN

Tyre Fryer
Matchbox by Lesney, 1972

29
JUN

Volkswagen Pick-up
Husky, 1967

30
JUN

Fourgon VW
Majorette, 1975

1
JUL

Transporter Vehicle
Matchbox, 1985

2
JUL

Rover MINI
Matchbox, 1972

3
JUL

Citroën DS
Siku, 1973

4
JUL

Mercedes-Benz ADAC LP 608 / Mercedes-Benz Pagode
Siku / Corgi Toys Juniors, 1974 / 1975

5
JUL

Mercury Commuter
Matchbox, 1969

6
JUL

Porsche 911 Turbo
Siku, 1981

7
JUL

Formula 5000
Matchbox by Lesney, 1975

8
JUL

VW Golf I
Majorette, 1980

9
JUL

VW Transporter Fire Truck
Siku, 1985

10
JUL

Dodge Challenger
Matchbox by Lesney, 1974

11
JUL

Saab 900 Turbo
Majorette, 1983

12
JUL

13
JUL

Inter-City Mini-Bus
Corgi Toys, 1971

Scammell Crusader
Matchbox by Lesney, 1973

14
JUL

Jaguar XK 120
Matchbox, 1984

15
JUL

Beach Buggy
Matchbox by Lesney, 1970

16
JUL

VW Transporter
Siku, 1985

17
JUL

Ford 17M Turnier Fire Engine
Siku, 1970

18
JUL

Ford Pick-up
Matchbox by Lesney, 1970

19
JUL

VW Passat Police
Siku, 1981

20
JUL

Wildcat Dragster
Matchbox by Lesney, 1970

21
JUL

Mercedes-Benz Studio
Schuco, 1948

22
JUL

Opel Rekord 1900 Coupé
Dinky Toys, 1968

23
JUL

Texaco Ford K-16 Truck
Matchbox Superkings, 1973

24
JUL

Soopa Coopa
Matchbox by Lesney, 1972

25
JUL

Porsche 911 Police
Siku, 1978

26
JUL

Roller
Siku, 1980

27
JUL

VW Bulli T1 Ambulance
Märklin, 1955

28
JUL

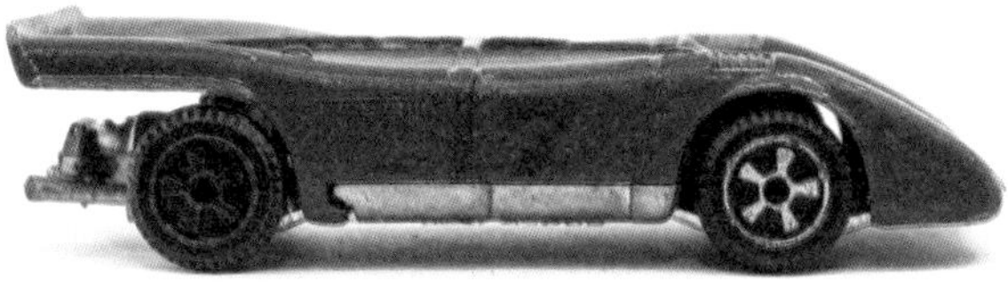

Porsche 917
Politoys, 1971

29
JUL

VW Bus T2 Camper
Matchbox, 1970

30
JUL

Foden Cement Mixer
Matchbox by Lesney, 1968

31
JUL

Ferrari Monza GT
Kirk Denmark, 1972

1
AUG

Mercedes-Benz 250 SE Police
Siku, 1975

2
AUG

Porsche 910
Märklin, 1966

3
AUG

K31-Pantone
Matchbox by Lesney, 1972

4
AUG

Ice Cream Canteen
By Lesney, 1963

5
AUG

Lancia Beta Montecarlo
Majorette, 1983

6
AUG

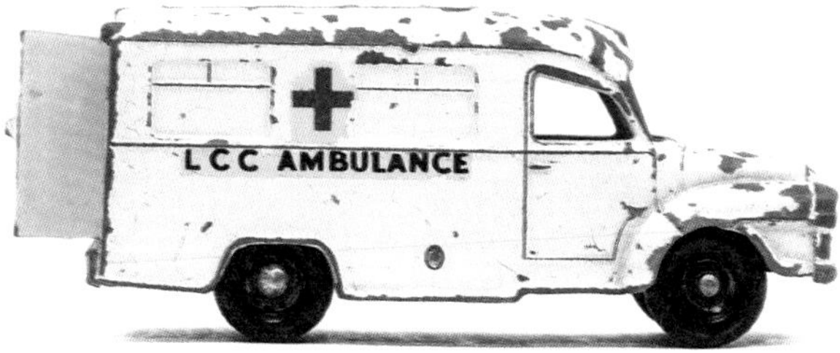

Bedford Lomas Ambulance
By Lesney, 1962

7
AUG

Dodge Trucks
Matchbox, 1971

8
AUG

Studebaker Lark Wagonaire
Matchbox by Lesney, 1963

9
AUG

Ford Tractor
Matchbox by Lesney, 1967

10
AUG

Lincoln Continental
Matchbox by Lesney, 1965

11
AUG

Audi 100 Coupé
Schuco, 1970

12
AUG

Lamborghini Countach
Bburago, 1988

13
AUG

Guy Warrior Car
Matchbox by Lesney, 1967

14
AUG

Opel Rekord Caravan
Siku, 1971

15
AUG

VW Käfer 1303 LS Cabriolet
Siku, 1989

16
AUG

Renault 4
Dinky Toys, 1962

17
AUG

Buick Regal
Corgi Toys Juniors, 1977

18
AUG

SAAB Sonett III
Matchbox by Lesney, 1973

19
AUG

Fourgon
Majorette, 1981

20
AUG

Porsche 910
Matchbox by Lesney Superfast, 1970

21
AUG

FAUN Crane Truck
Siku, 1979

22
AUG

Porsche 917/10
Siku, 1979

23
AUG

VW Bucket Car
Siku, 1980

24
AUG

VW Käfer 1302
Corgi Toys Toys, 1969

25
AUG

K-13 DAF Trucks
Matchbox Superkings, 1970

26
AUG

Road Dragster
Matchbox by Lesney, 1970

27
AUG

Willys Jeep
Corgi Toys Whizzlewheels, 1970

28
AUG

Porsche 911 Police
Siku, 1980

29
AUG

Jaguar E-Type
Corgi Toys, 1964

30
AUG

Opel Rekord Coupé
Siku, 1970

31
AUG

Jeep CJ5
Corgi Toys, 1980

1
SEP

Paperbone
Politoys, 1976

2
SEP

Jaguar XJ6
Husky Models, 1970

3
SEP

Vintage Metal Car
ZZ Germany, 1975

4
SEP

Mercedes-Benz 'Binz' Ambulance
Matchbox by Lesney, 1965

5
SEP

Coca Cola Peterbilt Truck
Matchbox by Lesney, 1978

6
SEP

Mercedes-Benz 450 SEL
Matchbox by Lesney, 1979

7
SEP

Range Rover Police Patrol
Matchbox, 1975

8
SEP

Ferrari Berlinetta
Matchbox by Lesney, 1963

9
SEP

Range Rover
Majorette, 1982

10
SEP

DAF Tipper Container Truck
Matchbox by Lesney, 1975

11
SEP

VW Käfer 1302
Majorette, 1975

12
SEP

MAN Bus
Siku, 1982

13
SEP

Ford GT 40
Siku, 1970

14
SEP

Porsche 924 / Musketeer Caravan
Corgi Toys / Tekno, 1985 / 1972

15
SEP

VW Polo
Corgi Toys Juniors, 1979

16
SEP

Porsche Carrera 6
Corgi Toys, 1969

17
SEP

Bedford Chupa Chups Red Truck
Liedo, 1988

18
SEP

Mercdes-Benz 350 SL
Majorette, 1980

19
SEP

Bobby Car
Big Simba-Dickie, 2012

20
SEP

VW Porsche 914
Siku, 1975

21
SEP

Porsche 911 Targa
Corgi Toys Whizzlewheels, 1975

22
SEP

Jaguar E-Type
By Lesney, 1964

23
SEP

VW Passat
Siku, 1981

24
SEP

K-32 Shovel Nose
Matchbox Superkings, 1971

25
SEP

Mercedes-Benz 240 D
Corgi Toys, 1974

26
SEP

FAUN Firefigher Crane
Siku, 1985

27
SEP

VW Polo
Corgi Toys, 1978

28
SEP

VW 411
Schuco, 1970

29
SEP

F1 Ferrari
By Lesney, 1962

30
SEP

Flipper
Matchbox by Lesney, 1973

1
OKT

Simca 1100 TI
Majorette, 1975

2
OKT

Isu Grifo
Matchbox, 1973

3
OKT

VW Käfer ADAC
Siku, 1979

4
OKT

FAUN Metz Airport Firefighter
Siku, 1975

5
OKT

Buick Riviera
Hot Wheels, 1971

6
OKT

Roll Royce Silver Cloud
Matchbox by Lesney, 1958

7
OKT

Porsche 917
Super Champion, 1974

8
OKT

Ford Taunus 15 M
Siku, 1969

9
OKT

Peugeot 205Turbo
Matchbox, 1983

10
OKT

Formula One
Matchbox by Lesney, 1971

11
OKT

Porsche 911 Turbo
Matchbox, 1978

12
OKT

VW Bus
Siku, 1976

13
OKT

Ford Escort
Corgi Toys Juniors, 1978

14
OKT

Carabo Bertone
Solido, 1968

15
OKT

BMW CSI 3.0
Majorette, 1975

16
OKT

Citroën CV2
Dinky Toys, 1966

17
OKT

Fire Chief Ford Galaxie
By Lesney, 1966

18
OKT

Zettelmeyer Loader EUROP
Siku, 1967

19
OKT

Porsche 911 Targa
Märklin, 1970

20
OKT

Madzda RX7
Matchbox, 1982

21
OKT

Kremer Porsche
Matchbox Turbo Specials, 1984

22
OKT

Refuse Truck King Size
Matchbox by Lesney, 1965

23
OKT

Porsche 928
Matchbox, 1979

24
OKT

Hi-Tailer
Matchbox by Lesney, 1974

25
OKT

Scania Vabis
Tekno, 1969

26
OKT

Mercury Cougar
By Lesney, 1968

27
OKT

Mercedes-Benz 250 SE Police
Siku, 1974

28
OKT

Ferrari F40
Matchbox, 1980

29
OKT

Mercedes-Benz Unimog U406
Siku, 1980

30
OKT

Ford Sierra
Majorette, 1988

31
OKT

Ford Zephyr 6
By Lesney, 1963

1
NOV

Corvette
Hot Wheels, 2004

2
NOV

Toyota Land Cruiser
Majorette, 1982

3
NOV

Citroën Acadiane Post
Majorette, 1981

4
NOV

Mercedes-Benz 250 SE
Siku, 1966

5
NOV

K-14 Scammel Freight Liner
Matchbox Superkings Lesney, 1975

6
NOV

Lamborghini 400 GT Espada
Siku, 1972

7
NOV

Porsche 356
Märklin, 1964

8
NOV

Opel GT
Siku, 1970

9
NOV

Matchbox Truck
Matchbox, 1981

10
NOV

Iso Grifo 7 Litres
Corgi Toys Whizzlewheels, 1972

11
NOV

Ford Group 6
Matchbox by Lesney, 1969

12
NOV

Renault 4 Police
Edition Atlas, 2016

13
NOV

Mercedes-Benz 280 SL
Corgi Toys Juniors, 1975

14
NOV

Ford Cortina Taunus
Matchbox by Lesney, 1979

15
NOV

Porsche 924
Corgi Toys, 1985

16
NOV

K20 DAF Truck / Lamborghini Espada 400 GT
Matchbox Superkings Lesney / Siku, 1971 / 1972

17
NOV

Mercedes-Benz 500 SEC Coupé
Siku, 1981

18
NOV

Audi 100
Siku, 1974

19
NOV

Mercedes-Benz 190 D Police
Siku, 1965

20
NOV

BMW 3.0 CSI
Matchbox by Lesney, 1974

21
NOV

Magirus
Majorette, 1980

22
NOV

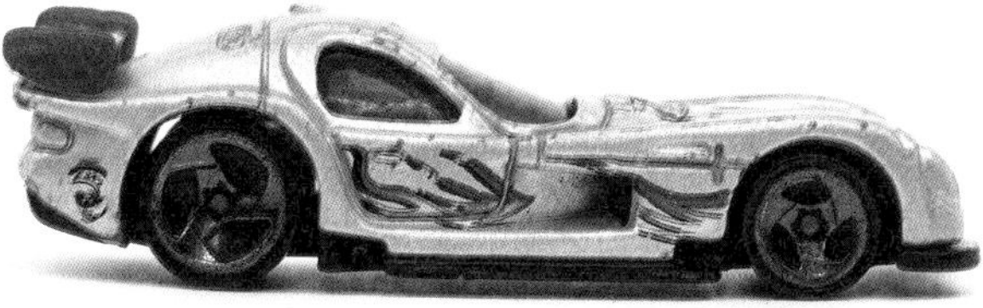

Panoz DTR
Hot Wheels, 1997

23
NOV

Fire Brigade Pompiers
Majorette, 1973

24
NOV

Ford F 500
Siku, 1971

25
NOV

K-5 MUIR HILL
Matchbox Superkings, 1972

26
NOV

Alfa Carabo
Matchbox by Lesney, 1970

27
NOV

Mercedes-Benz 250 SE Taxi
Siku, 1970

28
NOV

VW Bulli T2 Flatbed Truck
Siku, 1976

29
NOV

US-Ambulance
Matchbox by Lesney, 1977

30
NOV

Land Rover 109
Corgi Toys Whizzlewheels, 1965

1
DEC

Mod Tractor
Matchbox by Lesney, 1972

2
DEC

Mercury Commuter
Matchbox Superfast, 1971

3
DEC

Lone Star Truck

4

DEC

Lamborghini Marzal
Matchbox by Lesney, 1969

5
DEC

Blaze Buster
Matchbox by Lesney, 1975

6
DEC

VW Karmann Ghia Coupé
Märklin, 1967

7
DEC

VW Käfer 1300 Saloon
Matchbox by Lesney, 1976

8
DEC

Toe Joe
Matchbox by Lesney, 1972

9
DEC

Oldsmobile Toronado
Siku, 1970

10
DEC

VW Käfer 1302
Majorette, 1979

11
DEC

Iso Grifo
Matchbox Superfast, 1973

12
DEC

Renault 5 Turbo
Bburago, 1985

13
DEC

Mercedes-Benz Unimog U406
Siku, 1980

14
DEC

Ford Escort
Siku, 1972

15
DEC

BMW 3.5 CSL DTM

16
DEC

Porsche 924
Majorette, 1981

17
DEC

Lamborghini Espada 400 GT
Siku, 1972

18
DEC

Opel Kadett
Gama, 1982

19
DEC

Binz-EUROP Ambulance 1200L
Siku, 1974

20
DEC

VW Käfer 1303
Tonka, 1975

21
DEC

Ford Granada Turnier 2.3 GLS
Siku, 1982

22
DEC

Morgan
Majorette, 1983

23
DEC

VW Bulli T2
Welly, 2012

24
DEC

Lamborghini Marzal
Dinky Toys, 1968

25
DEC

Porsche 924
Corgi Toys, 1985

26
DEC

Fozzie Bear Car
Corgi Toys, 1979

27
DEC

Citroën 2CV Rallye
Majorette, 1976

28
DEC

Lamborghini Countach
Hot Wheels, 1987

29
DEC

Porsche 356
Maisto

30
DEC

Opel Rekord Caravan
Siku, 1971

31
DEC

IMPRINT

CHILDHOOD HEROES

Publisher seltmann+söhne
Zillestr. 105A, D-10585 Berlin
www.seltmannundsoehne.de

Art Direction
Stefan Küstner, seltmann+söhne

Printed in Germany
Seltmann Printart, Lüdenscheid
www.seltmann.de

All type designations for the cars were compiled carefully
and to the best knowledge and certain.

ISBN 978-3-946688-65-5